BORIS
The Shitting Buffalo

AARON CLAREY   JORGE E. GONZALEZ

Copyright © 2013 Aaron Clarey and Jorge E. Gonzalez
Published by Paric Publishing
Without limiting the rights under copyright reserved above, no part of this publication may be reproduced, stored in or introduced into a retrieval system, or transmitted, in any form or by any means (electronic, mechanical, photocopying, recording or otherwise), without the prior written permission of both the copyright owner and the above publisher of this book.

INTRODUCTION

I was dating a Russian ballet dancer at the time and though she had a good command of the English language, there was one word that kept perplexing her. The word "shit." She didn't know whether it was a verb, a noun, a plural noun, an adjective, etc., and asked me to explain how we in America used the word "shit." I had to laugh a little bit, because if you think about it, the word "shit" can be anything. A noun, a verb, an adjective, and it can also be used in the past, present or future tense, making "shit" not only the most endearing word in the entire English language, but the most confusing one as well. Because of this I decided to write and draw her a cute little book called "Boris the Shitting Buffalo" which would have Boris (a Russian buffalo) come to the United States and learn about all the wonderful uses and meanings of the word "shit." I intended on giving it to her for her 30th birthday, but she opted to stand me up that night instead, allowing for me and my colleague Jorge to bring Boris to life for the reading public.

Boris the Shitting Buffalo

Boris was from Russia.
He was a Russian Buffalo

But when he got to the USA, he did not know where to go.

So he asked some New Yorkers,
"Where's a place that's hip?"
And The New York buffaloes said
"The Badlands are the shit!"

Boris sure liked shitting. In Russia he was the BEST!

So off to South Dakota he went
To shit his heart out in the West!

Like visiting Mount Rushmore.

And then clandestinely take a poo!

Boris went to Sturgis.

Though he proved better at shitting than playing Sturgis drinking games.

Boris would go hiking and summit Harney Peak!

And when hikers were not looking,
a shit Boris would sneak!

Boris went to Deadwood
He was calm-cool-good at poker

Boris went fossil hunting!

But the Badlands was his favorite
That is where Boris had his heart

So off to the Badlands he went
to defecate, poop and fart.

Sometimes Boris would shit fast.

Boris would shit when it was dusk.

Boris would shit when it was light.

Boris would shit when it was morning.
(Boris doesn't like mornings)

Boris would shit at night.

Boris would shit in the rain.

Boris would shit in the snow.

For he was Boris the Shitter!
    The world's best shitting buffalo.

The End

Made in the USA
Middletown, DE
25 October 2014